DEDICATION:

This book is dedicated to my dad and personal superhero, Roy W. Hooker III. He has consistently been a Godly example of the 3 P's in my life; never has a day passed when he didn't profess his love for our family, provide for our family, and protect our family financially, emotionally, and spiritually. The inspiration for this book came from his heart and his uncanny love of organizing everything. Everything! My dad decided to arrange his important documents all in one place, so when he passes away someday, our grieving world would be a teeny bit easier from a to-do list perspective. It soon became a treasured father-daughter collaboration, and a labor of love for us to create and share this version of his vision with all of you. It is my hope that someday, when your loved ones are grieving over you, they will experience a moment of peace because of this book and the fact that you professed, provided, and protected them as well.

~Suzanne Hooker

Every reasonable attempt was made to ensure the accuracy of information in this book. It is possible that mistakes were unintentionally over looked; therefore the reader must independently confirm any information on which reliance is needed. As such, the author and publisher make no warranties about the contents of this book, except that the author's desire was to help families during their grieving process.

TABLE OF CONTENTS

WHAT TO DO WHEN A LOVED ONE DIES

IMMEDIATELY UPON DEATH

- ☐ Obtain a legal declaration of death. If a doctor is not present, you will need to contact someone to do this.
- ☐ If the person dies at home without hospice care, call 911.
- ☐ If a do-not-resuscitate document exists, it's vital to have this available. Without it, paramedics will generally start emergency procedures and except where permitted to declare death, they will take the person to an emergency room for a doctor to make the declaration.
- ☐ Contact the deceased's doctor. Page 25
- ☐ Contact close family and friends. Page 29
- ☐ Arrange for care of dependents and pets (if any).
- ☐ Contact the deceased's employer (if employed). Page 81
- ☐ Ask about benefits.
- ☐ Company Life Insurance
- ☐ Any outstanding paychecks due

A FEW DAYS AFTER THE DEATH

- ☐ Organize the funeral and burial or cremation. Page 33
- ☐ Check to see if there is a prepaid burial and funeral plan. Page 33
- ☐ Ask a friend or family member to go with you to the funeral home.
- ☐ Prepare the obituary. Page 71
- ☐ If the deceased was in the military, religious group, or fraternal group be sure and contact them to see if there are any burial benefits, or if they may help or conduct the funeral services.
- ☐ Contact a friend or family member to help answer the phone, collect mail, throw out food and take care of any pets and water plants.

Notes

UP TO TEN DAYS AFTER THE DEATH

- ☐ Obtain death certificates (usually the funeral home will provide them). Get multiple copies, as you will need them for insurance, claims, titles, etc. Page 23
- ☐ Contact your attorney with the Will or take it to the proper county or city office to have it accepted for probate (*It is so much better to have your own attorney*). Page 27
- ☐ Open a Bank account so that the Estate's Executor can deposit all of the necessary funds. Contact your attorney to determine how and what funds should go into the bank account. Page 27
- ☐ Check with your attorney to determine the best way to transfer all of the assets and funds to the deceased's Estate and how to handle the probate issues.
- ☐ If the deceased lived alone, contact the police and ask them to keep a watch on the vacant house.
- ☐ Contact the deceased's bank with the proper papers (Will and Executor's power) to move and close bank accounts. Locate all of the Bank accounts and Safe Deposit Boxes. Page 13
- ☐ Check with your Accountant concerning filing a Final Tax Return or an Estate Tax Return should be filed. Page 39
- ☐ Contact the deceased's Financial Advisor to make sure you have accumulated all of the investments and holding.
- ☐ Call the deceased's Life Insurance Agent to file claims for all of the life insurance. Page 41
- ☐ If the deceased was a Veteran, contact the Veterans Affairs 800-827-1000 (www.va.gov) to stop any payments and ask about survivor benefits. They may help in the burial or provide some burial benefits. Page 69
- ☐ Contact Social Security 800-772-1213 (www.ssa.gov) to stop payment and ask about survivor benefits. Possible burial benefits. Page 95
- ☐ Contact the deceased's place, or places of work that was paying retirement benefits to see if there are survivor benefits. Page 47
- ☐ If there are any changes to be made to the deceased's accounts, contact: Page 93
    - ☐ Cable company
    - ☐ Electrical Company

Notes

- ☐ Phone Company
- ☐ Newspaper
- ☐ Post Office for change of address if applicable

Notes

CHECK LIST OF ITEMS TO DO

PREPARE AHEAD OF TIME "THE FINAL CHAPTER" FOR THE ONES YOU LOVE

Contact an attorney and have them draw up items recommended:

- ☐ **Will** - Page 27
    - Know where the Will is kept
    - The Attorney's contact information
- ☐ **Living Will** - Page 27
    - Know where the Living Will is kept
    - Directives for type of procedures both wanted and unwanted.
- ☐ **Do-Not-Resuscitate Order** - Page 27
    - Know where the Do-Not-Resuscitate Order is kept
    - Designed to direct health-care professionals not to perform CPR if the person's heart or breathing stops and restarting would not result in a meaningful life.
- ☐ **Durable Power of Attorney** - Page 27
    - Giving authorization to a support individual
- ☐ **Health Care Surrogate** - Page 27
    - Giving authorization to help by making Health decisions

Be prepared to take all of the documents with you if the individual is taken to the hospital. Ask your attorney if you should give any of them to the Hospital personnel ahead of time.

Determine ahead of time:

- ☐ The FUNERAL HOME - Page 33
- ☐ The Burial Site - Page 35
- ☐ Select and contact the ATTORNEY you will use for the Estate - Page 27
- ☐ Select and get in touch with a CPA ahead of time you will be using - Page 39

Notes

- ☐ Gather the Following Information:
- ☐ SOCIAL SECURITY information - Page 95
- ☐ EMPLOYMENT contact information - Page 81
- ☐ BANKING information - Page 13
- ☐ INSURANCE POLICIES - Page 41
    - Health Insurance Policies
    - Life Insurance Policies
    - Veterans Insurance Policies
    - Funeral Insurance
    - Mortgage Insurance
    - Worker's Comp Insurance (if accident)
    - Homeowner Insurance
    - Flood Insurance
    - Personal Articles Insurance
    - Umbrella/Liability Insurance
    - Auto Insurance
    - Long Term Care Insurance
    - Any Additional Insurance
- ☐ LANDLORD, ASSITED LIVING, NURSING HOME, etc. – Page 89
- ☐ VETERAN'S AFFAIRS – Page 69
- ☐ CREDIT UNIONS – Page 13
- ☐ COMPUTER LOGIN & PASSWORD information – Page 17
- ☐ CREDIT CARD information - Page 21
- ☐ DEATH CERTIFICATE information - Page 23
- ☐ DOCTORS - Page 25
- ☐ ESTATE INFORMATION - Page 27
- ☐ INCOME TAX RETURNS - Page 39
- ☐ INVESTMENTS - Page 55

Notes

Notes

BANKING/CREDIT UNION

The FIRST thing you do before notifying the newspaper or any other source is to transfer ALL of the money out of our accounts (do not close the accounts) in to an account in just survivor's name - otherwise the bank might freeze the account and hold the money until probate.

DO NOT take the deceased's name off any bank accounts for at least one year in case some checks/refunds come with his/her name on it.

Review several recent Bank Statements to determine if there are any automatic drafts coming out that you should stop.

List all of the Banks, Credit Unions and Money Accounts you have:

BANK ONE

Bank Name: ______________________

Name on account: ______________________

Bank Address: ______________________

Phone Number: ______________________

Account Number: ______________________

Checking/Savings: ______________________

Safety Deposit Box
Authorized Users: ______________________

Key Location: ______________________

BANK TWO

Bank Name: ______________________

Name on account: ______________________

Bank Address: ______________________

Phone Number: ______________________

Account Number: ______________________

Checking/Savings: ______________________

Safety Deposit Box
Authorized Users: ______________________

Key Location: ______________________

Notes

BANK THREE

Bank Name: ______________________

Name on account: ______________________

Bank Address: ______________________

Phone Number: ______________________

Account Number: ______________________

Checking/Savings
Account Number: ______________________

Safety Deposit Box
Authorized Users: ______________________

Key Location: ______________________

Notes

COMPUTER LOGIN AND PASSWORDS

One of the great challenges you will have is the ability to login to various accounts and know the passwords. One of the easiest ways to assure access to these accounts is to use a Password Program on the computer. There are several good ones out there, just make sure you select one you have faith in. I, personally, use ROBOFORM, but there are certainly others. Once you set up the program, all you need is to remember the MAIN log in password. If you write it down, keep it in a secure place.

The MASTER password for my program is written down and stored:

Computer Name/location: ______________________

Computer login ID: ______________________

Computer password: ______________________

Computer Name/location: ______________________

Computer login ID: ______________________

Computer password: ______________________

Computer Name/location: ______________________

Computer login ID: ______________________

Computer password: ______________________

Computer Name/location: ______________________

Computer login ID: ______________________

Computer password: ______________________

Notes

CREDIT BUREAU INFORMATION

To help avoid identity theft, send a copy of the deceased's Death Certificate to each of these three credit bureaus:

Equifax

Phone: 1-888-766-0008 Mail: PO Box 105139, Atlanta, GA 30348

Equifax Notes:

TransUnion

Phone: 1-800-680-7289 Mail: PO Box 2000, Chester, PA 19022

TransUnion Notes:

Experian

Phone: 1-888-397-3742 Mail: PO Box 4500, Allen, TX 75013

Experian Notes:

Notes

CREDIT CARDS

All adults should have at least one or more cards issued in their name.

Card Type	Bank Issuer	Card Number	Phone Number

Notes

DEATH CERTIFICATE INFORMATION

Full Legal Name: ______________________________

Address: ______________________________

Length of time at current residence: ______________________________

Occupation: ______________________________

Occupation location: ______________________________

Social Security Number: ______________________________

Armed Services: ______________________________

Date of birth: ______________________________

Birthplace: ______________________________

Father's Full Legal Name: ______________________________

Father's Birthplace: ______________________________

Mother's Full Legal Name: ______________________________

Mother's Maiden Name: ______________________________

Mother's Birthplace: ______________________________

Notes

DOCTORS

Dr. Name: ______________________________

Phone Number: ______________________________

Office Street Address: ______________________________

City: ____________ State: ________ Zip: ________

Specialty: ______________________________

Dr. Name: ______________________________

Phone Number: ______________________________

Office Street Address: ______________________________

City: ____________ State: ________ Zip: ________

Specialty: ______________________________

Dr. Name: ______________________________

Phone Number: ______________________________

Office Street Address: ______________________________

City: ____________ State: ________ Zip: ________

Specialty: ______________________________

Dr. Name: ______________________________

Phone Number: ______________________________

Office Street Address: ______________________________

City: ____________ State: ________ Zip: ________

Specialty: ______________________________

Notes

ESTATE INFORMATION

If you do not have a will when you die, state law and the courts may determine who will administer your estate, handle financial matters, and act as a guardian for your minor children. If you have a will, you decide. You should review your will every few years due to federal and state laws changing. If you move to another state, your marital status or family situation changes, or your beneficiary dies, your will could be affected.

Do You Have a Durable Power of Attorney? (Yes) (No)
Location: ______________________________

Do You Have a Living Will? (Yes) (No)
Location: ______________________________

Do You Have a Designation of Health Care Surrogate? (Yes) (No)
Location: ______________________________

Do You Have a Do Not Resuscitate Order? (Yes) (No)
Location: ______________________________

Do You Have a Will? (Yes) (No)
Date of will (mm/dd/yyyy): ______________________________
Location of will: ______________________________

EXECUTOR
Name: ______________________________
Phone: ______________________________
Street: ______________________________
City, State, Zip: ______________________________

WILL PREPARED BY
Name: ______________________________
Phone: ______________________________
Street: ______________________________
City, State, Zip: ______________________________

Location of all documents: ______________________________

Notes

FRIENDS & FAMILY TO CONTACT

If you arrange ahead of time for someone to call the list of friends and relatives, it will certainly make things easier for you. Print off a list of the following to be able to give to someone.

People Who Can Help Notify Friends & Family:

Name	Phone	Notes

Notes

Friends & family to notify:

Name	Phone	Circle One	Other
		Friend / Relative / Close Family / Other	
		Friend / Relative / Close Family / Other	
		Friend / Relative / Close Family / Other	
		Friend / Relative / Close Family / Other	
		Friend / Relative / Close Family / Other	
		Friend / Relative / Close Family / Other	
		Friend / Relative / Close Family / Other	
		Friend / Relative / Close Family / Other	
		Friend / Relative / Close Family / Other	
		Friend / Relative / Close Family / Other	
		Friend / Relative / Close Family / Other	
		Friend / Relative / Close Family / Other	
		Friend / Relative / Close Family / Other	
		Friend / Relative / Close Family / Other	
		Friend / Relative / Close Family / Other	
		Friend / Relative / Close Family / Other	
		Friend / Relative / Close Family / Other	
		Friend / Relative / Close Family / Other	
		Friend / Relative / Close Family / Other	
		Friend / Relative / Close Family / Other	
		Friend / Relative / Close Family / Other	
		Friend / Relative / Close Family / Other	
		Friend / Relative / Close Family / Other	
		Friend / Relative / Close Family / Other	

Notes

FUNERAL ARRANGEMENTS

Organ Donor: (Yes) (No)

Funeral Visitation

Location: ______________________

Time: ______________________

Gathering after: ______________________

Funeral Service

Who will preside at the service?

____

Songs/Hymns:

____

____

____

Speakers/Pastor:

____

____

____

Flowers:

____

____

In lieu of flowers:

____

____

____

Notes

Pall Bearers:

1.
2.
3.
4.
5.
6.
7.
8.
9.
10.

Funeral Home:

Name:

Address:

Phone number:

Prepaid?

Burial Site:

Name:

Address:

Phone number:

Where to locate personal photos for my service:

Notes

Memorial Donation Suggestions:

Notes

Notes

INCOME TAX RETURNS

Income Tax returns are kept in this location:

CPA Firm:

CPA Name:

Phone Number:

Office Address:

City, State:

Zip:

Notes

Notes

INSURANCE

Contact each insurance agent and have the deceased's name removed from necessary policies. All of our polices are kept in this location:

____

____

____

Health Insurance:

Need to immediately call the deceased's health insurance company and inform them of his/her death.

Company Name: ______________________________

Phone Number: ______________________________

Policy Number: ______________________________

Life Insurance:

Contact your Life Insurance Companies or agent to file for benefits. Many Life Insurance policies were purchased before marriage and life's events took place. Be sure to review and update your Beneficiaries on all of your Life Policies.

When you file a Life Insurance Policy claim, you will direct the Life company how and where you want the money sent. Make sure you will receive one check per life policy.

Have the checks payable to:

Name: ______________________________

Address: ______________________________

Or - Have the checks sent to Electronically Transferred to:

Bank: ______________________________

Routing Number: ______________________________

Account Number: ______________________________

Notes

Notes

Life Insurance:

Life Insurance Company Name: ____________________

Agent's Name / Company: ____________________

Telephone Number: ____________________

Policy Number: ____________________

Policy Amount: ____________________

Primary Beneficiary: ____________________

Contingent Beneficiary: ____________________

Life Insurance Company Name: ____________________

Agent's Name / Company: ____________________

Telephone Number: ____________________

Policy Number: ____________________

Policy Amount: ____________________

Primary Beneficiary: ____________________

Contingent Beneficiary: ____________________

Notes

Life Insurance Company Name: ______________________

Agent's Name / Company: ______________________

Telephone Number: ______________________

Policy Number: ______________________

Policy Amount: ______________________

Primary Beneficiary: ______________________

Contingent Beneficiary: ______________________

Life Insurance Company Name: ______________________

Agent's Name / Company: ______________________

Telephone Number: ______________________

Policy Number: ______________________

Policy Amount: ______________________

Primary Beneficiary: ______________________

Contingent Beneficiary: ______________________

Accidental Life Insurance:

Insurance Company Name: ______________________

Telephone Number: ______________________

Policy Number: ______________________

Amount $: ______________________

Notes: ______________________

Notes

Veterans' Insurance:

Insurance Company Name: ______________________________

Telephone Number: ______________________________

Policy Number: ______________________________

Amount $: ______________________________

Notes: ______________________________

Employers or Pension Insurance – Survivor Benefits:

Insurance Company Name: ______________________________

Telephone Number: ______________________________

Policy Number: ______________________________

Amount $: ______________________________

Notes: ______________________________

Funeral Insurance:

Insurance Company Name: ______________________________

Telephone Number: ______________________________

Policy Number: ______________________________

Amount $: ______________________________

Notes: ______________________________

Notes

Mortgage and/or Credit Insurance:

Insurance Company Name: ______________________

Telephone Number: ______________________

Policy Number: ______________________

Amount $: ______________________

Notes: ______________________

____

____

Workers' Compensation Insurance (*In case death was accidental*):

Insurance Company Name: ______________________

Telephone Number: ______________________

Policy Number: ______________________

Amount $: ______________________

Notes: ______________________

____

____

Homeowners/Renters Insurance:

Insurance Company Name: ______________________

Telephone Number: ______________________

Policy Number: ______________________

Amount $: ______________________

Notes: ______________________

____

____

Notes

Flood Insurance:

Insurance Company Name: ______________________

Telephone Number: ______________________

Policy Number: ______________________

Amount $: ______________________

Notes: ______________________

____

____

Personal Articles Insurance:

*Review the personal article policy and remove necessary items.

Insurance Company Name: ______________________

Telephone Number: ______________________

Policy Number: ______________________

Amount $: ______________________

Notes: ______________________

____

____

Umbrella/Liability Insurance:

*Remove deceased person's name & vehicle once sold.

Insurance Company Name: ______________________

Telephone Number: ______________________

Policy Number: ______________________

Amount $: ______________________

Notes: ______________________

____

____

Notes

Auto Insurance:

*Do <u>NOT</u> cancel auto policy until deceased's vehicle is sold.

Insurance Company Name: ____________________

Telephone Number: ____________________

Policy Number: ____________________

Notes: ____________________

____

____

Any Additional Policies Not Listed Above:

Type of Insurance: ____________________

Company Name: ____________________

Telephone Number: ____________________

Policy Number: ____________________

Notes: ____________________

____

____

Type of Insurance: ____________________

Company Name: ____________________

Telephone Number: ____________________

Policy Number: ____________________

Notes: ____________________

____

____

Notes

INVESTMENTS

Investment Policies are another area you want to check today and make sure your Beneficiaries are correct. Many are years old, some before a Trust might have been set up and some after.

My Financial Advisor is:

Name of Company: ______________________________

Advisor's Name: ______________________________

Phone Number: ______________________________

Office Street Address: ______________________________

City, State. Zip: ______________________________

My Financial Advisor is:

Name of Company: ______________________________

Advisor's Name: ______________________________

Phone Number: ______________________________

Office Street Address: ______________________________

City, State. Zip: ______________________________

My Financial Advisor is:

Name of Company: ______________________________

Advisor's Name: ______________________________

Phone Number: ______________________________

Office Street Address: ______________________________

City, State. Zip: ______________________________

Notes

My Investment Company is:

Name of Company: ____________________

Advisor's Name: ____________________

Phone Number: ____________________

Office Street Address: ____________________

City, State. Zip: ____________________

My Investment Company is:

Name of Company: ____________________

Advisor's Name: ____________________

Phone Number: ____________________

Office Street Address: ____________________

City, State. Zip: ____________________

My Investments are with:

Investment Company: ____________________

Account Name: ____________________

Account Number: ____________________

Estimated Dollar Value: ____________________

As of Date: ____________________

Beneficiary: ____________________

Contingent Beneficiary: ____________________

Notes: ____________________

Notes

Investment Company: ______________________________

Account Name: ______________________________

Account Number: ______________________________

Estimated Dollar Value: ______________________________

As of Date: ______________________________

Beneficiary: ______________________________

Contingent Beneficiary: ______________________________

Notes: ______________________________

____

Investment Company: ______________________________

Account Name: ______________________________

Account Number: ______________________________

Estimated Dollar Value: ______________________________

As of Date: ______________________________

Beneficiary: ______________________________

Contingent Beneficiary: ______________________________

Notes: ______________________________

____

Investment Company: ______________________________

Account Name: ______________________________

Account Number: ______________________________

Estimated Dollar Value: ______________________________

As of Date: ______________________________

Beneficiary: ______________________________

Contingent Beneficiary: ______________________________

Notes: ______________________________

Notes

Investment Company: ______________________

Account Name: ______________________

Account Number: ______________________

Estimated Dollar Value: ______________________

As of Date: ______________________

Beneficiary: ______________________

Contingent Beneficiary: ______________________

Notes: ______________________

Notes

Notes

LONG TERM CARE

You should call immediately and cancel this policy – Do NOT cancel surviving spouse's policy, if one is available.

Location of Policy: ____________________

Company Name: ____________________

Agent Name: ____________________

Street Address: ____________________

City, State, Zip: ____________________

Phone Number: ____________________

Policy Number: ____________________

Notes

Notes

MARRIAGE CERTIFICATE

If you do not have a certified copy of the original Marriage Certificate, you may want to get one now as a certified copy is often required. Contact the Clerk of Court in the town in which you were married.

Location of Original Marriage Certificate

Notes

Notes

MEDICARE & MEDICAID

Copies of Medicare cards are located:

MEDICARE Supplement Policy is with:

Name of Company:

Advisor's Name:

Phone Number:

Office Street Address:

City, State. Zip:

Account Number:

Notes

Notes

MILITARY SERVICE

Branch of Service: ______________________

Service Serial Number: ______________________

Date Entered Service: ______________________

Place: ______________________

Type of Separation or
Discharge of Service: ______________________

Date: ______________________

Place of Separation: ______________________

Location of Military
Discharge Papers: ______________________

Highest grade, Rank, or
Rating Received: ______________________

Wars/Conflicts Served: ______________________

Additional information/Medals/Honors/Citations:

Notes

OBITUARY INFORMATION

FULL LEGAL NAME: ______________________

Age at death: ______________________

City: ______________________

State: ______________________

Day and Date of death: ______________________

Cause of death: ______________________

LIFE:

Birth date: ______________________

Birthplace: ______________________

Parents' Names: ______________________

Siblings' Full Name: ______________________

Siblings' Full Name: ______________________

Siblings' Full Name: ______________________

Siblings' Full Name: ______________________

Siblings' Full Name: ______________________

MARRIAGE:

Spouse's Name: ______________________

Married: ______________________

Place: ______________________

Notes

FAMILY SURVIVED BY (Name/Relation/Residence):

OTHER:

EDUCATION (School, College, University, etc.):

BRANCH OF SERVICE AND LENGTH OF TIME:

Notes

DESIGNATIONS, AWARDS, OTHER RECOGNITIONS:

EMPLOYMENT:

PLACES OF RESIDENCE:

HOBBIES:

Notes

CHARITABLE, RELIGIOUS, FRATERNAL ORGANIZATIONS:

OTHER:

LOCATION OF PHOTOS:

Notes

OBITUARY:

Notes

PLACE OF EMPLOYMENT

Contact place of employment and notify them of the deceased's death. If you are listed as the employee's beneficiary, it is important to contact the deceased's employer and ask about any possible death benefits, pension plans or retirement annuities, and health and life insurance coverage. Unions and other professional organizations may provide benefits also. Note: Sometimes you must return the deceased's final monthly pension payment to the pension company before they send a new, adjusted payment. If the deceased was employed, notify the employer.

Company Name: ______________________________

Person To Speak With: ______________________________

Address: ______________________________

Phone Number: ______________________________

Notes

Notes

PROPERTY

HOME/RENTAL:

Address: ______________________________

City, State: ______________________________

IN A TRUST: (Yes) (No)

Financial Institution	
Name:	______________________________
Address:	______________________________
City, State, Zip:	______________________________
Phone Number:	______________________________
Paperwork location:	______________________________

MORTGAGE: (Yes) (No)

Financial Institution	
Name:	______________________________
Address:	______________________________
City, State Zip:	______________________________
Phone Number:	______________________________
Paperwork location:	______________________________

Notes

Vehicle 1 (Car, Boat, RV, etc.):

Vehicle: ______________________

Financed in Who's Name: ______________________

Financial Institution: ______________________

Phone Number: ______________________

Title & Registration location: ______________________

Notes: ______________________

____

Vehicle 2 (Car, Boat, RV, etc.):

Vehicle: ______________________

Financed in Who's Name: ______________________

Financial Institution: ______________________

Phone Number: ______________________

Title & Registration location: ______________________

Notes: ______________________

____

Vehicle 3 (Car, Boat, RV, etc.):

Vehicle: ______________________

Financed in Who's Name: ______________________

Financial Institution: ______________________

Phone Number: ______________________

Title & Registration location: ______________________

Notes: ______________________

____

Notes

Vehicle 4 (Car, Boat, RV, etc.):

Vehicle: ____________________

Financed in Who's Name: ____________________

Financial Institution: ____________________

Phone Number: ____________________

Title & Registration location: ____________________

Notes: ____________________

____

Vehicle 5 (Car, Boat, RV, etc.):

Vehicle: ____________________

Financed in Who's Name: ____________________

Financial Institution: ____________________

Phone Number: ____________________

Title & Registration location: ____________________

Notes: ____________________

____

Vehicle 6 (Car, Boat, RV, etc.):

Vehicle: ____________________

Financed in Who's Name: ____________________

Financial Institution: ____________________

Phone Number: ____________________

Title & Registration location: ____________________

Notes: ____________________

____

Notes

Notes:

____

____

____

____

____

____

____

____

____

____

____

____

RESIDENCE INFORMATION IF NOT A HOMEOWNER:

Apartment	
Complex Name:	______________________
Contact Phone Number:	______________________
Contact Person:	______________________
Copy of Lease is located:	______________________
Paperwork location:	______________________
Lease Start Date:	______________________
Lease End Date:	______________________
Deposit Amount:	______________________

Notes

Senior Living Complex

Complex Name: ____________________

Contact Phone Number: ____________________

Contact Person: ____________________

Copy of Lease is located: ____________________

Paperwork location: ____________________

Lease Start Date: ____________________

Lease End Date: ____________________

Deposit Amount: ____________________

Assisted Living Complex

Complex Name: ____________________

Contact Phone Number: ____________________

Contact Person: ____________________

Copy of Lease is located: ____________________

Paperwork location: ____________________

Lease Start Date: ____________________

Lease End Date: ____________________

Deposit Amount: ____________________

Notes

SERVICES & SUBSCRIPTIONS

Contact the following to change or stop service:

POWER

Company Name: ______________________

Phone Number: ______________________

Account Number: ______________________

PIN #: ______________________

WATER

Company Name: ______________________

Phone Number: ______________________

Account Number: ______________________

CABLE

Company Name: ______________________

Phone Number: ______________________

Account Number: ______________________

NEWSPAPER

Company Name: ______________________

Phone Number: ______________________

Account Number: ______________________

MAIL

Company Name: ______________________

Phone Number: ______________________

Account Number: ______________________

Notes

SOCIAL SECURITY INFORMATION

Social Security Administration
Windsor Park Building
6401 Security Blvd.
Baltimore MD 21235
1-800-772-1213 / www.ssa.gov

Social Security benefits are not automatically paid; a survivor must apply for them. In order to apply, the survivor needs to complete and submit several documents to the Social Security Administration office within a specific amount of time. A lump sum payment may be made when an eligible person passes away. This payment is only made if there is an eligible surviving widow, widower, or entitled child. Survivor's check may go to certain members of the worker's family.

An application for the lump sum death payment should typically be made within two years of the worker's death. Do not delay the application process because you do not have all of the information required. The people in the Social Security office will advise you about other proof of information options can be used.

It's advised to check your record every three years to verify the earnings are being correctly reported to your record.

You will need the following information when you contact the Social Security Office to collect benefits:

- ☐ Certified copy of death certificate
- ☐ Social Security Number of the survivor and the deceased
- ☐ Survivor's birth certificate
- ☐ Marriage Certificate (if the survivor is the widow)
- ☐ Survivor's proof of US citizenship or lawful alien status if born outside the US
- ☐ Divorce papers if applying as a surviving divorced spouse
- ☐ Children's Birth Certificates and social security numbers (if applicable)
- ☐ Deceased worker's W2 for previous two years or federal self-employment tax return
- ☐ Proof of widow age if 62 or older

Notes

☐ Survivor's bank and account number so benefits can be directly deposited

Deceased Social Security Number:

____

Social Security Card Location:

____

Notes

Taking the time now to complete this book will save your loved ones challenges, frustrations, and grief beyond measure. In death, just as in life, this will remind them of your love, your protection, and how you provided for them. It truly is a labor of love on your part, which they will forever appreciate.

Made in the USA
Monee, IL
30 November 2021

83537162R00059

The Final Chapter

Suzanne Hooker

Published by Prominence Publishing.
www.prominencepublishing.com

Publisher's Note: This is for educational and entertainment purposes only. This is not meant to represent legal, medical, or any other kind of professional advice. The reader should do his or her own due diligence and seek professional advice when required.

The Final Chapter / Suzanne Hooker. -- 1st ed.
ISBN: 978-1-988925-48-6